REAL LIFE MONSTERS

CANOPY
BOOKS

Written by Ed Masessa and Melanie Masessa
Designed by Scott Westgard
Illustrations by Leonardo Meschini and Andrea Morandi

© 2009 by Canopy Books, LLC
50 Carnation Ave.
Floral Park, NY 11001

ISBN-10: 1-607-43336-2
ISBN-13: 978-1-607-43336-1

Printed in China

TABLE OF CONTENTS

This book features some of the real-life monsters that occupy the world around us. They have **razor-sharp teeth, venomous fangs and stingers, and powerful jaws and claws**—and they don't mess around! They range in size from tiny to enormous, but when it comes to finding their next meal or protecting their territory, they are all capable of inflicting pain that can sting, paralyze, or kill.

WHEN YOU GO TO THE BEACH,
ARE YOU AFRAID TO GO INTO THE WATER?

WHEN YOU GO CAMPING, DO YOU **STRAY INTO THE DARKNESS**
BEYOND THE SAFE LIGHT OF THE CAMPFIRE?

IN THE WATER, YOU CAN'T SEE **WHAT LIES JUST BELOW THE SURFACE.**
IN THE DARKNESS, THERE ARE MANY THINGS THAT **CAN SEE BUT CAN'T BE SEEN.**

It doesn't matter to a snake or scorpion if you accidentally stick your hand into a leaf pile—
you will probably be bitten or stung.

It doesn't matter to a swarm of jellyfish that you didn't know they were there—
you might still pay for your mistake.

It doesn't matter to a SHARK that you aren't a seal—
you just might happen to look like one.

If you watch scary movies, you know that there are many kinds of monsters, both real and imaginary. The imaginary ones will play with your mind. But the real ones... they usually aren't interested in playing. For them, it's a world where only the strongest survive.

So the next time you feel like going for a swim or taking an evening walk in the woods, remember that you're entering another world— one in which **you may not be alone!**

VAMPIRE BAT

THE IMAGE OF TERRIFYING CREATURES SWOOPING DOWN OUT OF THE NIGHT SKY TO BITE YOUR NECK AND SUCK YOUR BLOOD IN A FEROCIOUS FRENZY IS ENOUGH TO GIVE EVEN THE BRAVEST PERSON A NIGHTMARE. The vampire bat is indeed a blood sucker—well... actually more of a drinker. And it does swoop out of the night sky, but it's not exactly ferocious. And it's not even very big, but it looks so incredibly nasty!

While the wingspan of the vampire bat is about 7 inches (17.8 centimeters), its body is only as big as a human's thumb and weighs about 2 ounces (57 grams).

The vampire bat has heat sensors in its nose that help it to locate a vein on its prey's skin, and its grooved tongue is very efficient at lapping up blood. The **bite** is harmless, but it can cause serious infections. The animal has a chemical known as **draculin** in its saliva that prevents the blood from clotting. The vampire bat will drink for about 30 minutes and consume half of its body weight in blood— about 2 tablespoons.

THE VAMPIRE BAT LIVES IN COLONIES OF MORE THAN 100 TO SEVERAL THOUSAND. IT IS FOUND IN MEXICO, CENTRAL AMERICA, AND SOUTH AMERICA.

Vampire bats will sleep in very dark places during the day and emerge at night to feed. Their favorite targets? Sleeping cows and horses. When the vampire bat feeds, **it silently drops out of the darkness** and lands near its victim. Then it walks on all fours over to the sleeping animal, uses its razor-sharp teeth to pierce the skin, and licks up the blood that drips out.

Bats are the only mammals that can fly. There are more than 900 species of bats, and vampire bats are among the **SMALLEST**!

The vampire bat finds its prey using **echolocation**, or biological sonar—like dolphins and whales. This is also similar to sonar used on ships. The bat sends out a signal, which hits an object and "echoes" back to the bat, telling it where the object is.

THE SCIENTIFIC NAME FOR THE BAT KNOWN AS THE FLYING FOX IS **PTEROPUS VAMPYRUS**. NO WONDER WE'RE CONFUSED!

Vampire bats are the only mammals to feed entirely on blood. This is known as **hematophagy**.

KOMODO DRAGON

THE WORD "DRAGON" IS DERIVED FROM THE LATIN *DRACO*, MEANING "SERPENT." Dragons evoke visions of monstrous winged, scaly creatures breathing fire and flying off with cows grasped in their deadly talons. This real-life dragon may not have wings or breathe fire, but make no mistake—it's just as deadly!

Living in isolation on remote islands, Komodo dragons only became known to the western world in 1910. They are the perfect example of island gigantism—that's where the dominant predator on an isolated island will get larger with each generation.

This carnivore is the largest living species of lizard. It is found only on the Lesser Sunda Islands in Indonesia. These harsh, arid, volcanic islands are now part of Komodo National Park, where the Komodo dragon is a protected species.

It can grow to 10 feet (3.1 meters) in length and weigh more than 300 pounds (136 kilograms). Its tail is as long as its body. These lizards are excellent swimmers and are frequently seen swimming from island to island.

The Komodo dragon will eat almost anything. It's mainly a scavenger that feeds on carrion (rotting meat), which it can smell up to 5 miles (8 kilometers) away. But it will also eat a live meal, such as deer or pigs and occasionally humans! It can eat up to 80 percent of its body weight in one feeding.

The Komodo dragon deserves every bit of its fearsome reputation. A **PATIENT HUNTER**, it lies perfectly still while unsuspecting prey walks past. Then it attacks, ripping into the throat or soft underbelly of the victim.

There are only about 4,000 left in the wild, making it an endangered species. Attempts to breed Komodo dragons in zoos have been somewhat successful, but there is a long way to go.

The Komodo dragon has long, **sharp claws** and about 60 **serrated teeth** used for ripping and tearing chunks of meat that it swallows whole. After it has digested its meal, the Komodo dragon will regurgitate something similar to a gigantic owl pellet, full of hair and teeth, and covered in mucus.

It has a **long, yellow, forked tongue** that it uses to detect taste and smell. Its saliva is loaded with bacteria. So even if an animal survived the initial attack, it would soon die from infection.

YOUNG KOMODO DRAGONS LIVE IN TREES. IF THEY DIDN'T, CHANCES ARE THEY WOULD GET EATEN BY AN ADULT!

HIPPOPOTAMUS
"RIVER HORSE"

THE HIPPO IS A VERY DECEPTIVE CREATURE—FROM ITS BLOOD RELATIVES (WHALES) TO ITS SPEED AND INTELLIGENCE. There are only two species left in existence—the Common and the Pygmy—and with their current rate of decline, they might not be around too much longer.

The Ultimate Sleepwalker

Hippopotamuses are able to sleep underwater. Every five minutes or so, they rise to the surface and take a gulp of fresh air—without waking up!

The hippopotamus will spend up to 16 hours every day **SUBMERGED IN WATER** to help keep its body cool. Its eyes and nose are high on its head so that it can see and hear while most of its body remains underwater. It can hold its breath underwater for five to six minutes before resurfacing for air.

They live in eastern, central, and southern Africa and are endangered. Along with being hunted and loss of habitat, they give birth only every two years.

Hippopotamuses live in groups called either herds (like cows) or pods (like dolphins). Like the elephant seal, the male hippopotamus is called a bull and the female a cow, but the baby is a calf. Calves are born underwater like whales and manatees, and they weigh about 100 pounds (45 kilograms).

Even on land, a hippopotamus can outrun the average human for the first few hundred yards, achieving speeds of 20 to 30 miles per hour (32 to 48 kilometers per hour). While the calf can swim quite well, the adult hippopotamus does more of a skip and bounce along the river bottom.

They are the **third-largest land mammal** behind the elephant and rhino. They weigh between 5,000–8,000 pounds (2,268–3,629 kilograms) and are approximately 5 feet (1.5 meters) tall and 10-14 feet (3-4.3 meters) long.

Sweat blood?

When the hippopotamus relaxes on the shore, it sweats. What looks like blood is actually a protective oil that acts as part sunscreen and part antibacterial lotion.

They are one of the **most aggressive** animals in Africa. Their enormous mouth, teeth, and tremendous size make them extremely dangerous. They will attack crocodiles as well as humans. A small boat offers little protection.

ARCTIC LION'S MANE JELLYFISH

IMAGINE YOU ARE SWIMMING ALONG THROUGH FRIGID WATERS WHEN SUDDENLY YOU SMACK INTO A 6-FOOT (1.8-METER) WALL OF GELATINOUS GOOP. Then your arms, legs, and torso start to burn as invisible tendrils brush against you, casually injecting you with bits of venom. You have just had a close encounter with a large lion's mane jelly!

The box jelly, also known as the sea wasp, is the **most venomous animal in the world**! More than 5,000 people have died from its venom in the past 60 years. And even if you survived an attack, you're in incredible pain for weeks afterward.

These jellies live in the cold waters of the **northern Atlantic and Pacific Oceans**, as well as the Arctic Ocean. They eat fish, plankton, and other sea jellies. Because of their long, sticky, stinging tentacles, they usually do not have to swim to catch their prey.

The color of the lion's mane jelly is determined by its size. Larger ones are shades of dark red and purple, while smaller ones are light orange or tan.

The lion's mane jelly has no bones or cartilage, no heart, no blood, no brain, are made up of 95 percent water, and cannibalize other jellies. Jellyfish are not actually fish, which is why scientists and aquariums prefer to use the term **sea jellies**.

It is called a lion's mane jelly because of its resemblance to the distinctive display of hair found on male lions.

Even a tentacle that is no longer attached to a jellyfish can sting. In humans, contact with a tentacle can cause pain, skin rashes, fever, and muscle cramps. Vinegar will neutralize the toxins.

Jellyfish have been around for more than **650 MILLION YEARS**.

THE STING FROM THE TENTACLES MAY ALSO BE A DEFENSE MECHANISM AGAINST THE LION'S MANE'S PREDATORS, LIKE SEA TURTLES AND LARGE FISH.

The lion's mane jelly has **nearly-invisible tentacles** grouped into eight clusters, and the number of tentacles ranges from 500 to 1,200. These tentacles are filled with paralyzing venom that is injected into the victim.

Measured from the top of its "umbrella" to the tip of its longest tentacle, it is **the largest animal on Earth**. They can grow to 120 feet (36.6 meters) in length—even longer than a blue whale. Their bell, or body, can grow up to 8 feet (2.4 meters) across and is divided into eight lobes, which makes it look like an eight-pointed star when viewed from above.

EMPEROR SCORPION

THE EMPEROR SCORPION, ALSO KNOWN AS THE IMPERIAL SCORPION, IS ONE AWESOME CREATURE! Try to imagine sleeping under the stars, relaxing to the tune of crickets chirping, when you look down and crawling up your sleeping bag is an emperor scorpion, like a creature out of an *Indiana Jones* movie!

The emperor scorpion grows to be 8 inches (20 centimeters) long and has a life span of six to eight years. These scorpions are very popular as pets because of their size and beauty.

Females have about 10-20 babies per litter. They are born white and molt several times, getting darker each time. They are called scorplings, and for the first few months, they ride on Mom's back.

Tastes like chicken? Maybe! The emperor is edible once you've removed the stinger segment of the tail (the telson) that contains the venom. It's a good source of protein.

The scorpion's color ranges from black to dark blue to dark brownish-green. But it's fairly easy to find at night. A handheld black light will make the emperor glow bright green!

Despite the scorpion's size, its snap is worse than its sting. Only people who are allergic to its **VENOM** will have a reaction to being stung. To everyone else, it will feel like a bee sting. But the **PINCERS** are very powerful and can inflict major pain.

The emperor can be found in the west-central countries of Africa. It lives in burrows that it digs in dark places. It is nocturnal and quite shy, mostly coming out just to hunt for food.

This scorpion looks like a lobster, but actually, it's related to the spider. It belongs to the scientific class Arachnida along with spiders, mites, and ticks.

THIS CREATURE HAS MANY ENEMIES BESIDES HUMANS, INCLUDING MONKEYS, BIRDS, REPTILES, SPIDERS, AND RODENTS.

When threatened, the scorpion will face its opponent, spread its pincers wide, and arch its formidable stinger high over its back. This impressive stance is enough to scare off some predators.

ALLIGATOR SNAPPING TURTLE

It has three pronounced ridges of spiked plates running the length of its shell. Combine this unique feature with the massive head, powerful jaws, and thick, scaled tail, and it's easy to see why this creature is called the dinosaur of the turtle world!

IF YOU WERE WALKING ALONG A RIVERBANK OR SMALL CREEK IN FLORIDA OR LOUISIANA, YOU MIGHT THINK YOU HAVE TIME-TRAVELED TO THE AGE OF THE DINOSAURS. This is one turtle you don't want to meet in a dark alley! The alligator snapping turtle is the largest freshwater turtle in North America, and quite possibly the world. Males are much larger than females and can weigh up to 200 pounds (91 kilograms) and live to be 100 years old! It lives in the waterways of the southeastern United States and will spend almost its entire life in the water, where it feeds on fish, snakes, amphibians, and rotting carcasses.

Females lay up to **50 eggs** about 150 feet (46 meters) from the shoreline. The eggs are deposited in a hole that the turtle has dug. The temperature of the eggs will determine whether the baby that hatches is male or female.

The alligator snapping turtle is built for **camouflage**. Along with its black, brown, and dark green color, it's covered in algae, making it nearly invisible to unsuspecting fish.

HUMANS are their only predators. They are killed for their meat and unique shell.

GOTCHA!

The alligator snapping turtle has a bright red piece of flesh attached to the tip of its tongue that looks like a worm. The turtle lies at the bottom of a lake with its mouth open and wiggles its tongue like a fishing lure to attract fish, then SNAP!

Alligator snapping turtles are not usually aggressive to humans, but don't make them feel threatened—and definitely don't try to pick them up! Their powerful jaws can easily amputate a person's finger.

COLOSSAL SQUID

The squid is a **CEPHALOPOD**, a class of mollusks that includes octopuses and cuttlefish. As with all cephalopods, the squid uses jet propulsion to move.

SEA MONSTERS WITH SUCKER-LINED ARMS OF GIGANTIC PROPORTIONS, CIRCLING THE BODIES OF SAILORS, AND DRAGGING THEM FROM THEIR SHIPS INTO THE DEEP. The colossal squid is responsible for many of these tales. This marine monster lives in the cold, deep waters of the ocean and, until recently, the only specimens scientists had to work with were the remains of dead squid. In the past few years, research crews have photographed the colossal squid in its natural habitat. And fishermen have unwittingly snared squid in their nets. But we still know very little about this giant of the deep, which poses such questions as, what if the 40-50-foot (12-15-meter) beasts discovered are only babies?

The colossal squid thrives in cold water more than 3,000 feet (914 meters) deep where very little sunlight can penetrate. Hence, because they live in relative darkness, this squid's eyes are larger than those of any other creature on Earth. Measuring between 10-12 inches (25.4-30.5 centimeters) in diameter, they are about the size of a basketball!

Colossal Squid vs. Giant Squid

While these terms might be used interchangeably, they refer to two distinctly different species. The colossal squid, with its bigger mantle, has more mass. The giant squid, with longer arms and tentacles, has greater overall length. The largest squids found have measured 45-60 feet (13.7-18.3 meters) in total length and weigh up to a ton. That's about as long as one-and-a-half school buses, and as heavy as 11 adult men!

One of the squid's best defense mechanisms is its ability to change color to match its surroundings, thereby becoming virtually invisible. Its special skin cells, called chromatophores, react and change in a split second.

There are about 500 species of squid, and all have **eight arms and two longer tentacles** armed with hooks and suckers. The suckers are mounted on stalks and are ringed with a hard material called chitin that allows them to bite into their prey.

AS IF DEADLY HOOKS AND SUCKERS AREN'T ENOUGH, THE SQUID HAS A PARROT-LIKE BEAK THAT RIPS ITS FOOD INTO SMALL PIECES.

Another defensive device at the squid's disposal is **ink**. When threatened, the squid will emit an inky blob resembling its general shape. Its enemy confused, the squid then has time to rocket itself to safety.

Has a colossal squid ever attacked a human?

Not yet. But humans are overfishing one of its favorite foods—the Patagonian toothfish, commonly known as Chilean sea bass. Eventually, the squid may have to find another food source. To that 12-inch (30.5-centimeter) eyeball, a crowded summertime beach might look like a bag of buttered popcorn!

CLASH OF THE TITANS

The first evidence of the existence of the colossal squid was found in the stomachs of sperm whales. A sperm whale will aggressively attack this super-sized meal. It is not known if the squid will attack first, but sucker scars on the whale's hide indicate the squid puts up a tremendous fight for survival. These ferocious battles result in certain death for one, and sometimes both, of the warriors.

MAPS OF ANCIENT MARINERS OFTEN REFER TO SEA MONSTERS THAT ATTACK SAILING VESSELS. AMONG THOSE MYTHS IS THE KRAKEN, A LEGENDARY DEEP-SEA MONSTER SO LARGE IT WAS OFTEN MISTAKEN FOR AN ISLAND.

SPERM WHALE

The only non-human predators of sperm whales are ORCAS—killer whales—and even they will only attack the baby calves once they have separated from their mothers.

THE SPERM WHALE IS A MARINE MAMMAL. THIS AMAZING GIANT OF THE SEA IS THE LARGEST TOOTHED WHALE. There are other, larger whales that have baleen instead of teeth, like the blue whale. In the 18th and 19th centuries, sperm whales were ruthlessly hunted for their meat and oil and were listed as an endangered species. They are now protected and beginning to make a comeback. Between 200,000 and 350,000 roam the ocean depths in all five oceans of the world.

The sperm whale population will eat more seafood in a year than the entire human population. One whale eats 2,000 pounds (907 kilograms) of squid and fish every day.

Partially because of the lack of sunlight in the ocean depths, whales use **echolocation** for locating objects and prey. This is the same system a bat uses and is also similar to sonar used on ships. The whale sends out a signal that hits an object and "echoes" back to the whale, telling it where the object is.

WOW Whale Facts!

- The heart can weigh almost 300 pounds (136 kilograms).

- Each tooth is about 7 inches (17.8 centimeters) long—that's almost as tall as this book!— and weighs 2 pounds (1 kilogram).

- It has the largest brain of any creature—20 pounds (9 kilograms)!

A fully-grown bull can weigh an amazing **90,000 pounds** (40,823 kilograms) and grow to **60 feet** (18.3 meters). That's 1½ times the length of a school bus!

Its dark gray skin is usually covered with circular **SCARS** from battles with colossal squid.

Whales travel in groups called pods, which can have between 10 and 20 members. A baby whale, or calf, will stay with the pod for about 10 years. An adult male is called a bull and an adult female is called a cow.

In 1820, the 87-foot- (26.5-meter-) long whaleship *Essex* set sail from Nantucket, Massachusetts, on a two-and-a-half-year voyage. While the crew was busy killing members of a pod of sperm whales, a large bull rammed the ship twice and sank it. This incredible battle was immortalized in 1851 by Herman Melville, who wrote the classic story of the great white whale, Moby Dick.

In March 2007, a sperm whale strayed into a small cove off the coast of Japan. As rescuers tried to herd it back to open waters, it suddenly turned on them, capsizing the boat and killing one fisherman.

This whale has a very **unique jaw**. The lower jaw has 20-25 teeth on each side, but the upper jaw has openings that the lower teeth slide into.

ANACONDA

THE FIRST EUROPEAN EXPLORERS TO VISIT THE JUNGLES OF SOUTH AMERICA BROUGHT BACK TALL TALES OF MONSTROUS, MAN-EATING SNAKES THAT COULD POISON A MAN WITH THEIR BREATH.

Stare into their eyes, and you'd be hypnotized! These snakes are neither venomous nor hypnotic, but these tales of the anaconda probably emerged because when you're running away from something much bigger and stronger than you are, it's hard to give an accurate description.

An anaconda has teeth but is **not venomous**. It will bite its prey to hold it still while it quickly coils around the animal, squeezing the life out of it. Prey either suffocate or drown, but are not crushed. The snake will then unhinge its jaw and swallow the animal whole!

Anacondas have the largest size difference between males and females of any vertebrates (animals with backbones). Females are five times bigger!

They eat mostly birds, fish, mammals, and reptiles. The bigger they are, the bigger their meal. They have been seen eating deer and jaguars and have even been reported to devour humans! In 2005, a 13-foot (4-meter) Burmese python was found in the Everglades. It attempted to swallow a 6-foot (1.8-meter) gator before its stomach ruptured.

They live close to water in the tropics of **South America**, including Ecuador, Columbia, Venezuela, Brazil, Bolivia, and Peru.

Anacondas are mainly NOCTURNAL (active at night). They like to hunt in the water, but will also lie in trees and drop on unsuspecting prey.

While anacondas average about 20 feet (6.1 meters) in length and have the diameter of a grown man, there have been reports of specimens up to 35 feet (10.7 meters) long and weighing more than 500 pounds (227 kilograms). It's extremely difficult to measure one since they're not easy to get out of the water.

Their olive-green skin, patterned with oblong black splotches, gives them the perfect camouflage both in the water and on land.

Anacondas give birth to live young that are immediately on their own. In contrast, pythons lay eggs and care for them.

The anaconda is the largest snake in the world by mass, taking into account size and weight. The Asiatic reticulated python is longer, but much slimmer.

GREAT WHITE SHARK

ONE OF THE MOST FEARED CREATURES ON EARTH, THE GREAT WHITE SHARK LIVES AND ATTACKS IN THE COASTAL WATERS ALL OVER THE WORLD. This carnivorous fish has been around for 100 million years, but it isn't the biggest or fiercest shark on record. That honor goes to the prehistoric Megalodon that was an amazing 50 feet (15.2 meters) long!

The great white has been known to exceed 20 feet (6.1 meters) in length and weigh a whopping 4,500 pounds (2,041 kilograms).

It has a **sharp sense of smell.** A single drop of blood can be detected in an Olympic-sized swimming pool. Their smell is directional, meaning both their left and right nasal cavity can function independently, which also enables them to rapidly pinpoint the location of prey.

While many sharks are found on exhibit in aquariums, you will not find a great white among them. They are extremely difficult to keep alive in captivity and therefore we don't really know how long they live.

JAWS

This famous 1975 movie about a great white shark terrorizing and devouring members of a small island community made for terrific horror but wasn't entirely accurate. Great white sharks will attack and bite humans, but they don't actually eat them. Human flesh cannot be digested because the flesh-to-bone ratio is too low.

The skeleton is composed of **cartilage**, which keeps the body lightweight for rapid movement and prevents the shark from sinking to the ocean floor. This is the same flexible material that is found in our noses and ears. Their lightweight frame allows swimming speeds estimated to be 15 to 25 miles per hour (24 to 40 kilometers per hour).

Their TEETH are all the same shape; they only vary in size.

Several rows of **triangular teeth** that can number in the thousands create a bite that is twice as strong as a lion's. With one chomp, a great white can consume up to 30 pounds (13.6 kilograms) of flesh. They do not chew their food. They hold the prey in their serrated teeth and rattle their head back and forth, sawing through and tearing off pieces of flesh.

Its white belly, from which its name is derived, allows the great white to blend with the sky when viewed from underneath. From above, the gray coloration **camouflages** it with the surrounding ocean, making it look like no more than a shadow.

Great whites prefer a fatty meal in their diet, which includes fish, dolphins, sea turtles, whales, seals, and sea lions.

Baby great whites are about 4.5 feet (1.4 meters) in length, weigh 50 to 60 pounds (23 to 27 kilograms), and unlike humans, are born with a full set of teeth.

TASMANIAN DEVIL

THE CARTOON CHARACTER KNOWN AS TAZ ISN'T FAR OFF FROM THE REAL THING! While the real-life Tasmanian devil doesn't spin like a tornado, it does run around in circles and it is known to throw a temper tantrum when it feels threatened, making it an awesome beast to be reckoned with.

It is the largest carnivorous **marsupial** in the world and lives only on the island of Tasmania off the southeast coast of Australia. Its lifespan is about eight years. Marsupials are mammals that have pouches on their bellies in which they carry their young.

Unlike the kangaroo, the pouch where the devil carries her babies faces backward. This is to protect the babies from dirt as the mother burrows with her front claws. Other diggers like the wombat also have this feature.

The devil has very long whiskers on its snout and head that help it locate prey, and it has a very developed sense of smell. **These creatures will eat an entire animal—** flesh, bones, fur, and all! While they mostly like to eat carrion, they will also hunt for live prey.

It is the size of a small dog but looks more like a small bear with its stout body, black fur, and thick neck. It is about 3 feet (0.9 meters) long from head to tail and weighs between 18 and 22 pounds (8.2 and 10 kilograms).

The reputation of the devil is well earned. When angry or threatened, its ears will turn from pink to red, it will release a powerful, skunk-like odor, and it will make the most awful shrieking, snorting, grunting noises you will ever hear.

The devil is active from DUSK UNTIL DAWN and sleeps during the day in hollowed logs or beneath large rocks.

It has a large head with extremely powerful jaws. Pound for pound, the devil is the most powerful biter in the animal world.

The devil was almost hunted into extinction but became a **protected species** in 1941. However, a contagious disease called Devil Facial Tumor Disease (DFTD) is spreading rapidly in the wild. It causes large tumors that eventually cause the devil to starve to death.

A devil will give birth to several dozen raisin-sized babies, but only four can eat at any one time, so most don't survive. Babies crawl up and into the pouch, where they live for the next 15 weeks.

GOLIATH BIRD-EATING SPIDER

THEY ARE SNEAKY, CREEPY, AND FAST. Every movement of their eight legs has the appearance of a threat, as if you are being stalked. What's not to fear when it comes to spiders? Now imagine your average-sized house spider inflated to about the size of a base on a baseball field. Or try lying down, taking a dinner plate, and placing it on your chest—that's how the goliath bird-eater would look as it was crawling up your sleeping bag. Now there's a reason to stay up all night!

When feeling threatened, it will rear up in an awesomely frightening pose. It will flick **urticating hairs** from its body through the air toward the potential threat. These tiny, almost invisible hairs are exceptionally irritating to human skin.

Native tribes roast and eat these large spiders as a good source of protein. After dinner, the fangs are even used as toothpicks!

Its lungs are called "book lungs" because they look like the pages of a book.

SPIDER SHAKE

These giant tarantulas do not have teeth for tearing and chewing—**their mouths are nothing but straws**. In order to eat, they regurgitate (throw up) digestive juices onto their victims, which make mush out of the soft inner tissues and create a tasty shake for the spider to slurp up. All that remain in the end are fur, feathers, and skeleton.

The goliath bird-eater is the **largest spider in the world**. It can reach a leg span of 12 inches (30.5 centimeters) and weigh as much as a quarter-pound hamburger! It lives in the hot, humid rainforests of South America. It is related to the emperor scorpion.

It also wards off impending th... ts by making a loud hissing noise, which it does ... g the bristles on the legs together. This is can ... ulation and can be heard up to 15 feet (4.6 met ers) away!

The goliath will live up to 15 years. Females lay up to 400 eggs at a time, which then hatch into **SPIDERLINGS**.

They live in burrows and come out at night to hunt. Like a tiger, the goliath bird-eater will sneak up and pounce on its prey, overpower it, and inflict one fatal bite using its venomous fangs.

One of its natural enemies is the tarantula hawk. This spider wasp is about 2 inches (5.1 centimeters) in length with long legs that have grappling hooks at their tips. The tarantula hawk will sting the spider, paralyze it, and drag it back to its nest. Then it lays eggs on the goliath that burrow into the spider, eating it alive!

While they have been seen eating small birds, they usually feed on lizards, frogs, insects, and rodents. Their venom is **not fatal to humans**, but getting pierced by fangs that can be up to an inch (2.5 centimeters) long is very painful.

GREAT BARRACUDA

ONE MINUTE YOU ARE SCUBA DIVING, OBSERVING THE COLORFUL LIFE FORMS OF A CORAL REEF, AND THE NEXT MINUTE YOU ARE STARING DOWN THE POINTED HEAD OF A 6-FOOT (1.8-METER) TORPEDO WITH TEETH! Where did it come from, and how did it sneak up on you so quickly? The great barracuda is a vicious predator that uses incredible bursts of speed to sneak up on its prey. This creature can accelerate up to 30 miles per hour (48.3 kilometers per hour) in a second. By comparison, world record holder Michael Phelps swims at a top speed of under 6 miles per hour (9.7 kilometers per hour).

As an adult it has few predators, but younger ones can fall victim to sharks and large fish like tuna.

It has a torpedo-shaped body and a strong tail—
the perfect combination for RAPID ACCELERATION.

This saltwater fish is found around the world in tropical and subtropical oceans.

Part of the barracuda's fierce reputation comes from its toothy grin, which is caused by a severe underbite—the lower jaw protrudes further than the upper jaw, leaving the fangs exposed.

IT HAS BEEN KNOWN TO SKYROCKET 20 TO 30 FEET (6.1 TO 9.1 METERS) OUT OF THE WATER AND INTO THE BOATS OF FISHERMEN, INFLICTING SOME NASTY BITES IN THE PROCESS.

As with another great predator, the great white shark, the barracuda is bluish-gray on top with a white belly. It also has several dozen dark stripes and has earned the nickname "Tiger of the Sea."

The great barracuda can grow up to 6 feet (1.8 meters) long and weigh 110 pounds (50 kilograms). It has an insatiable appetite for fish, which it will impale and snap in half with its dagger-like teeth.

MEKONG GIANT CATFISH

THE MEKONG RIVER, THE 12TH LONGEST RIVER IN THE WORLD, IS HOME TO THE LARGEST NUMBER OF BIG FISH ON THE PLANET. There are more than 1,000 species of fish in the Mekong River, several of which grow to amazing proportions. But because it is so rich in aquatic life, it is also heavily fished to feed the growing human population of the region. How long will these big fish last?

The peoples of the Mekong River system believe the giant catfish to be a sacred fish. In Cambodia, this fish is called trey reach, which translates to **"royal fish."**

While the Mekong giant is considered to be freshwater, scientists have discovered that it is actually anadromous, which means it spends some of its life in the ocean and travels to freshwater areas to breed. Migration routes have been recorded with distances reaching up to 600 miles (966 kilometers) inland.

This giant herbivore lives in the murky brown waters of the Mekong River in Thailand, Laos, Cambodia, and Vietnam, where it eats plants and algae on the river bottom.

It has one of the fastest growth rates of any fish in the world, capable of reaching up to 400 pounds (181 kilograms) in just six years.

As with all catfish, the Mekong giant has no scales; a large, flattened head; and a wide mouth that enables it to feed through suction. This fish is also **NEGATIVELY BUOYANT**, meaning it usually sinks.

Over the past century, populations are reported to have declined 95 percent, and the Mekong giant is now classified as **endangered**. It is fighting an uphill battle against humans. Habitat destruction, overfishing, and other manmade intrusions such as dams near its breeding grounds are literally killing its chances for survival.

Would you like that super-sized? The Mekong giant catfish is one of the largest freshwater fish in the world. It is capable of reaching up to 10 feet (3 meters) in length and 650 pounds (295 kilograms). That's about the size of a grizzly bear!

It is born with teeth but loses them within the first few years, after which it gums its food to death. The **lack of teeth** makes it easy to tell the Mekong giant from other catfish.

ELEPHANT SEAL

It's called an elephant seal because of the large, pendulous, **trunk-like snout** on the bull, which is very important during mating season. The bull uses his "trunk" to make loud roaring noises. The "trunk" also helps the bull to conserve moisture during the mating season when he rarely leaves the beach for food and takes in very little water.

IF YOU WERE ONE OF THE 30 OR SO PEOPLE WHO LIVE ON MACQUARIE ISLAND, ABOUT HALFWAY BETWEEN AUSTRALIA AND ANTARCTICA, YOU WOULD DEFINITELY BE IN THE MINORITY. Along with the thousands of penguins and fur seals that call this island home, there are approximately 70,000 elephant seals.

The seals gather in large groups called colonies on land, and in smaller groups called rafts in the water. Their breeding grounds are called rookeries.

Despite its size, the elephant seal's torpedo shape makes it a **swift swimmer**. They will dive between 2,000-4,000 feet (610-1,219 meters) down in search of food like squid, eel, penguins, and rays. Their unique anatomy allows them to hold their breath underwater for up to two hours.

They were hunted to the brink of extinction in the 1800s for their very thick blubber, which was boiled down into lamp oil. Blubber is a layer of fat that keeps the seal warm in frigid water temperatures.

Elephant seals are pinnipeds—marine mammals that include seals, sea lions, and walruses that live mostly in water, but go on land to rest and have babies. They spend about 80 percent of their time in the water.

While elephant seals have 32 TEETH, most of them are flat. Only the upper and lower canine teeth are sharp. Rather than chew their food, they swallow it whole.

The bulls will wage **FEROCIOUS BATTLES** to determine which will be the dominant (or alpha) male in the colony.

The elephant seal is the **largest species of carnivore**. The males, or **bulls**, will grow up to 20 feet (6.1 meters) long and weigh more than 10,000 pounds (4,536 kilograms). Females, or **cows**, are slightly smaller. Babies are called **pups** and weigh 75-80 pounds (34-36 kilograms) at birth and grow to 300 pounds (136 kilograms) in a month!

There are two species: the **northern elephant seal** is found in California and the Baja peninsula. The larger **southern elephant seal** is found in Antarctic waters.

ITS ONLY NATURAL PREDATORS ARE KILLER WHALES, LARGE SHARKS, AND HUMANS.

WOLVERINE

THE WOLVERINE HAS BUILT UP A FIERCE REPUTATION, SPREAD MOSTLY BY RUMORS PASSED ON THROUGH GENERATIONS OF HUMANKIND. They are not really the breaking-and-entering type, but just like that kid in your class who gets a reputation for being a troublemaker, when a cabin in the woods gets raided, the wolverine gets the blame.

It can be found in Alaska, **Canada**, and **Russia** in the forests and tundra regions where the human population is low and interaction is kept to a minimum.

The wolverine will bury a carcass for later in the winter when food becomes scarce. Its jaws are **strong enough** to crush bones, rip apart frozen meat, and even **chew through a steel cage.**

Baby wolverines are called **kits.** Between one and three kits are born at a time in a den that is dug deep into the snow—a snow cave! Only one pound (0.45 kilograms) at birth, they grow to almost the size of an adult in the first year.

When threatened, it will give off an **incredible stench.** Combine this with the fact that it looks similar to a skunk, and you'd think they are related—but they're not!

The wolverine is the largest terrestrial (land-dwelling) member of the weasel family. The only family member that is larger is the giant otter that lives in South America. Other relatives include ferrets, minks, and badgers.

It has powerful jaws and long, sharp claws that it uses very effectively to defend itself as well as its food. It usually scavenges for food but will kill what it needs to survive—squirrels and rabbits, but occasionally something as big as a moose!

The wolverine is really **A LONER** who prefers to live in very remote areas because it needs a lot of room to roam around. Other than humans, its only natural predator is the wolf.

The wolverine's fur is protected by "guard hairs." These long, coarse hairs protect the undercoat from frost accumulation. This is the reason the fur was so valued by trappers and why it is used to line parkas.

Its fur is dark brown with a yellow-gold stripe that runs from shoulder to tail along its sides. It will grow up to 45 inches (114 centimeters) and 60 pounds (27 kilograms), about the size of a medium dog with a long tail. The females are much smaller than the males.

Its muscular body and short legs resemble that of a small bear with a long tail. Many years ago, trappers gave it the nickname "**Devil Bear.**"

MORAY EEL

KNOWN AS A COSMOPOLITAN SPECIES, WHICH MEANS THEY ARE FOUND ALL OVER THE WORLD, THERE ARE MORE THAN 100 SPECIES OF MORAY EELS THAT LIVE IN THE TROPICAL AND TEMPERATE SEAS. They come in an amazing variety of colors, but don't be fooled; these predators are lightning-fast and extremely menacing!

They range in size from 2 ½ inches (6.4 centimeters) to 12 feet (3.7 meters) and can live up to 35 years.

The moray is **nocturnal** and **carnivorous**. It eats mostly fish and cephalopods, like squid and octopus. And it doesn't matter if its prey is dead or alive!

The moray is typically seen with its jaws open. It has very small gills and needs to constantly open and close its jaws to help it "breathe." Because of this, even the inside of the mouth is camouflaged!

MORAY EELS HAVE SMALL EYES AND VERY POOR EYESIGHT SO IT'S DIFFICULT FOR THEM TO KNOW HOW BIG THEIR FOOD IS. IT'S NOT UNCOMMON FOR A MORAY TO BITE OFF THE FINGERS OF THOSE WHO ARE FEEDING THEM!

The dragon moray is one of the most impressive specimens with its black, white, yellow, orange, and red in a dragon-like pattern. It has **HUGE FANGS**, a **POINTED SNOUT**, and **HORNS** above its eyes, and it's one of the most aggressive morays.

One of the most amazing features of the moray is a second set of jaws called **pharyngeal jaws**. As the eel bites onto prey, this retractable jaw lunges forward, bites again, and drags the prey down the eel's throat.

Moray eels have **incredibly sharp teeth** that are slanted inward for tearing into the flesh of their prey.

You are what you eat! The moray feeds on fish that have eaten toxic algae. This toxin (**CIGUATOXIN**) builds up in the moray but doesn't harm it. However, it makes the eel extremely toxic to humans. In 1135, King Henry I died after eating a toxic eel.

The **patterns** and **colors** of moray eels would make the most famous fashion designers jealous! They are speckled and freckled, striped and solid, in brown, black, yellow, blue, and every color in between.

The moray eel prefers to hang out in nooks and crevices of **coral reefs** where only their heads are exposed. Although it has a vicious reputation, it is actually shy and will only attack if threatened.

CROCODILE

PEOPLE TEND TO SPEAK OF ALLIGATORS AND CROCODILES AS IF THEY WERE INTERCHANGEABLE. IF YOU WERE BITTEN BY EITHER, THE RESULT WOULD BE THE SAME—AND IT WOULDN'T BE PLEASANT. The most apparent physical difference is the shape of the snout, which is long and narrow on a croc, but wider and U-shaped on a gator. Crocs are also lighter in color and can tolerate salt water more easily. But the croc is also the more aggressive—you could say, it's the "real-life monster."

Gators are found only in the southeastern US and parts of China, but the croc is found all over the world throughout the tropics. If zoos did not have breeding programs, the Chinese alligator might become extinct within a few years.

A nearly complete fossil of a super-sized croc that lived more than 100 million years ago was found in the Sahara Desert. It was estimated to be 40 feet (12.2 meters) in length and weighing 20,000 pounds (9,072 kilograms).

When swimming, they tuck their legs against their bodies, making them more streamlined. And their feet are webbed to help them change direction quickly when chasing prey.

The largest species is the saltwater crocodile found in North Australia and Southeast Asia. The largest croc on record was 28 feet (8.5 meters) long and almost 3,000 pounds (1,361 kilograms). The smallest species is the dwarf crocodile, which "only" grows to about 5 feet (1.5 meters).

Say Ahhh... While many lizards can flick their tongues in and out, the croc can't. Its tongue is fixed to the inside of its bottom jaw by a piece of skin.

The croc's lineage dates back more than 200 million years, which means they somehow **SURVIVED THE GREAT DINOSAUR EXTINCTION EVENT!** You could say they are the cockroach of the reptile world.

Crocs have excellent night vision— something that works against them when being hunted by humans. The same layer in their eyes that helps them see at night also reflects light, making the eyes glow red in the beam of a flashlight.

Because of the croc's powerful jaw muscles, its bite force is the strongest of any animal. The great white shark's bite force is about 400 pounds per square inch (2,758 kPa). The croc's... 5,000! CHOMP!

The muscles used to open its mouth are relatively weak, which is why its mouth can be held shut with duct tape. When a croc has its mouth closed, you can still see all of its teeth.

They eat fish, birds, and mammals and are excellent ambush hunters capable of bringing down wildebeests and zebras as they lunge out of the water. Saltwater and Nile crocodiles are the most dangerous species. They kill hundreds of people every year. To these monsters, a human washing clothes on a riverbank looks like a tasty treat!

GIANT MANTA RAY

THE 1968 NEWBERY HONOR-WINNING BOOK THE BLACK PEARL, BY SCOTT O'DELL, IS THE STORY OF A 16-YEAR-OLD BOY WHO BATTLES AN ENORMOUS DEVILFISH THAT GUARDS A RARE BLACK PEARL. Other stories have been written about this colossal, winged fish and have given it a frightening reputation. While its size is legendary, its reputation is quite misleading.

There are important differences between mantas and stingrays:

- Stingrays have a venomous stinger, while mantas do not.

- A stingray's mouth is located underneath the fish; the manta's mouth is in front.

- Stingrays eat mostly small fish and shrimp, and mantas eat mostly plankton.

Divers can often get very close to these gentle creatures. However, **touching them can hurt them**. They are covered with protective mucus that can be rubbed off easily, exposing their skin to infection. Their skin is covered with rough, tooth-like scales called **denticles** that feel like sandpaper.

The babies are called **pups**. They are born live and immediately take off on their own. The fact that they are about 4 feet (1.2 meters) long and weigh 100 pounds (45.4 kilograms) might have something to do with that!

On September 4, 2006, while filming a documentary, Steve "The Crocodile Hunter" Irwin was stabbed in the heart by a 200-pound (91-kilogram) bull ray's spine. The venom from a stingray contains a powerful nerve toxin that affects the heart. By injecting the venom directly into Steve's heart, the results were lethal.

Also called the **DEVIL FISH** or **BLANKET FISH**, it will live up to 30 years in tropical waters all around the world.

The small fish that are usually seen attached to the belly of the giant manta are **remoras** or **suckerfish** that tag along for the ride and eat scraps that get away. They do no harm to the manta.

The giant manta is the **LARGEST OF ALL THE RAYS**. It is known to grow up to 29 feet (8.8 meters) wide and weigh up to 5,000 pounds (2,268 kilograms)! Because of their enormous size, they are rarely kept in captivity.

The giant manta is harmless as it **swims majestically** through open water, but has earned a bad reputation because of its size. This creature's "wings" are actually super-sized pectoral fins. It swims by "flapping" them.

The giant manta also has large, lobe-like flippers called **cephalic fins** on either side of its mouth that help funnel plankton into its mouth. But these fins are actually extensions of the pectoral wings.

Sharks, mantas, skates, and stingrays are all part of the same scientific classification **Elasmobranchii**. What makes them similar is that they all have a skeleton made up of cartilage, not bone.

AUSTRALIAN FRILLED LIZARD

WHEN IT COMES TO THE WEIRD AND WONDERFUL WORLD OF ANIMALS, THERE IS NO PLACE ON EARTH LIKE AUSTRALIA. Some of nature's oddest curiosities have assembled here—and in some cases (like the platypus), it would appear they have been assembled. The Australian frilled lizard, a half-pint dragon of the woodlands, is no exception. And it has one of the best bluffs in all of nature.

The frilled lizard—also known as the **dragon lizard**—is an arboreal reptile, which means it lives most of its life in trees. This 3-foot (1-meter) reptile occupies the forest and woodlands of northern Australia.

THE FRILLED LIZARD DOES NOT DO WELL IN CAPTIVITY, AND IT RARELY HAS A CHANCE TO SHOW OFF ITS MOST UNIQUE FEATURE SINCE IT IS RARELY THREATENED IN A CAGE.

Its brown-gray skin gives it excellent camouflage against the bark of a tree. It is also very difficult to photograph in the wild. A **shy creature**, it will circle a branch or trunk to stay out of one's line of vision.

Despite its fierce appearance, it is quite **HARMLESS.**
The dragon costume is its only defense.

It has only a few natural predators— snakes, birds, larger lizards, and feral cats, an invasive species.

If the camouflage strategy doesn't work, it will pop open the frill, open its mouth, hiss, rear up on its hind legs, and lunge at the enemy.

While it is fairly safe in trees, it is exposed when it goes to the ground to feed. It eats insects, spiders, and other small lizards.

This amazing creature has a flap of skin around its throat that looks like a shawl. But when it feels threatened, the mouth opens wide, showing off sharp teeth. The shawl or frill pops open like an umbrella, revealing an impressive dragon-like collar that is almost 1 foot (0.3 meters) across, and its mouth and tongue are shocking shades of bright yellow and pink.

When it gets alarmed or it is threatened, it will try to act invisible using its skin as camouflage.

If all of its defense mechanisms fail to scare away its enemy, as a last resort, it turns around and runs on its hind legs for the nearest tree, where it can become invisible again. The display is so comical that it momentarily stuns predators.

LIONFISH

TAKE A TRIP TO AN AQUARIUM AND YOU WILL MORE THAN LIKELY SEE A CROWD AROUND THE TANK THAT CONTAINS THE LIONFISH, ONE OF THE MOST COLORFUL FISH IN THE OCEAN. Chances are also good that this fish will not have any company in the tank. It might only eat when it's hungry—but it's always hungry.

Although their venom **isn't deadly to humans**, it really hurts! The pain will last up to 30 minutes and linger for days afterward. Some side effects include burning pain and swelling around the sting, headaches, nausea, vomiting, and difficulty breathing.

The lionfish starts quite small but **grows very rapidly**, and soon outgrows its tank. Collectors have taken to dumping these fish into the ocean, and because they multiply quickly, eat ravenously, and have few natural predators, they are taking over ecosystems and causing severe economic and environmental harm.

It is also known as a **scorpion fish**, **turkey fish**, and **dragon fish**. It has long, separated spines and zebra-like stripes that are stunningly beautiful in bright shades of red, brown, white, yellow, and orange.

They will grow up to 15 inches (38 centimeters) in length with a fin-spread of 1.5 feet (0.46 meters), weigh 2.5 pounds (1.1 kilograms), and live up to 15 years. Relative to some of the monsters of the deep, their size seems to work against them, but the **venom in those spines packs one powerful punch!**

It is one of the most venomous fish in the ocean, but it will not aggressively attack. The lionfish's toxic spines are mainly used for defense. When threatened, it will lower its head and raise its spines forward in an intimidating pose.

In the blink of an eye, lionfish **SNATCH THEIR PREY** and swallow it whole before it even realizes it's in danger. They are extremely aggressive predators with insatiable appetites.

So why is it called a lionfish? The fierce hunting tactics of these fish are similar to lions. They will either ambush their prey with **lightning-quick strikes**, or use their large pectoral (side) fins to corral it.

It is extremely agile and uses its fins to **gracefully swim** in all different directions—especially when tracking down its next meal.

It eats mainly crab, fish, and shrimp and hunts during the hours of dusk and dawn when the dim light assists its natural **camouflage**.

What is the biggest **Real Life Monster?** In this book, a monster is defined as an animal that is either strange, terrifying, or unusually large for its kind. Some have jaws so strong they can bite through steel. Several are as big (or bigger!) than a school bus. And some are creatures straight out of a sci-fi movie—the things from which nightmares are made. But are these monsters real or imagined? After all, animals in the wild will kill what they need to survive—either for self-defense or for food—but they are mindful of another's territory. The old adage "Leave them alone and they'll leave you alone" holds true in almost every case.

However, if an alien race were to visit our planet to bring back a specimen of the baddest of the bad, it could very well choose a **HUMAN**. We have the most complex brains of any creature on Earth, yet we destroy entire ecosystems, upset the balance of nature, and endanger our planet in the process. Think about it...